Contents

 Assessment text

Burning Hope
page 2

Written by
Lou Kuenzler

Illustrated by
Nelson Evergreen

Series editor **Dee Reid**

Before reading
Burning Hope

Characters

Lena

Ricky

Sport Squad captain

Tricky words

ch1 p7	dunes	
ch2 p8	shuddered	
ch2 p10	sneered	
ch2 p10	furious	
ch2 p11	Egyptian	
ch3 p13	disbelief	
ch4 p19	stomach	
ch4 p20	glared	

Story starter

Two teams of young athletes were stranded on a desert island after a plane crash. Lena was a javelin thrower with North Athletic. The other team, Sport Squad, had divided the island in half and made each team hunt for food on their own side. North Athletic fetched branches to burn at night as a signal to passing ships.

Burning Hope

Chapter One

I was sitting on the beach watching the orange fire crackle in the dark. Tariq, the captain of our athletics team, had told us we must always keep the fire burning at night. The fire was a signal for planes and ships to show them we were stranded on this desert island.

Everybody in the team had fetched branches from the jungle all afternoon. It was hard work and it had been hot in the sun. It was good to sit quietly now in the cool night air.

I made a special wish. "Please, let there be a ship nearby," I whispered to myself. If a ship saw our fire, it could take us home. I suppose it could take our rival team, Sport Squad, as well. They do not like us, their captain is a bad-tempered bully and they even steal our food, but they should still be rescued.

I threw a branch onto the fire. It was my turn to stay up and keep the fire burning. Ricky, the team's shot thrower, was supposed to help me but he was sleeping.
CRASH!
I heard a sound in the bushes. A branch cracked.

"Ricky," I hissed.

He opened his eyes. I did not want him to think I was frightened, but I was pleased he woke up.

"What is it?" Ricky asked.

"I heard a noise," I said softly.

"I'm sure it's just a deer or a small animal," Ricky said.
"You're probably right," I replied. "I did see some rabbits in the dunes when I was hunting this morning."
Another branch snapped.
"That's a very loud noise for a rabbit," I said, but Ricky was already sleeping again.

Chapter Two

"Ricky, please get up," I whispered. Another branch cracked in the darkness. I was sure I could hear a creature hiding in the bushes. It was coming closer. I shuddered in fear and my heart was pounding.

I looked for my javelin. I knew it was lying on the sand where I had left it, but it was too dark to see anything on the ground.

"Ricky," I hissed, shaking his arm.
It was too late. Five boys from Sport Squad suddenly sprang out of the trees. Before Ricky even woke, the boys sprinted forward and grabbed us. They had a thin rope.

"Get off!" I screamed.
In the light of the fire, I saw the Sport Squad captain. He had a big white number one on his green vest.
"Leave us alone," growled Ricky.
"We don't have any food here for you to steal," I snapped.
"Ha!" the captain laughed. "We don't want your food this time. We want something even better than that."
"What?" I asked.
"Wait and see," sneered the captain.
Two boys lifted me, then dragged me across the sand. The other boys and the captain pulled and pushed Ricky. He was furious but it did no good. There were too many of them. They tied us back to back against a tall tree.

The rope was so tight I felt like an Egyptian mummy wrapped in bandages. I couldn't even move my arms. I twisted my legs and shoulders but it was useless. Ricky called loudly for help but I knew our team would not hear us. Our camp was too far away.

Chapter Three

"Why have you come over to our side of the island?" I shouted at the Sport Squad boys. I tried to scramble to my feet but the rope around me was too tight.

"If you're not after our food, then what do you want to steal?" cried Ricky, who was doing his best to escape from the rope that held him to the tree.

"Firewood, of course," grinned the Sport Squad captain. He pointed to the huge heap of branches our team had fetched that day. "We will take those back to our camp. Thank you for doing all the work for us," he laughed. "We have fresh meat that needs cooking."

"No!" I cried in disbelief. "You can't take that firewood. We have to keep this fire burning. It is a signal. If ships see it, they will come and rescue us. It's our only chance."

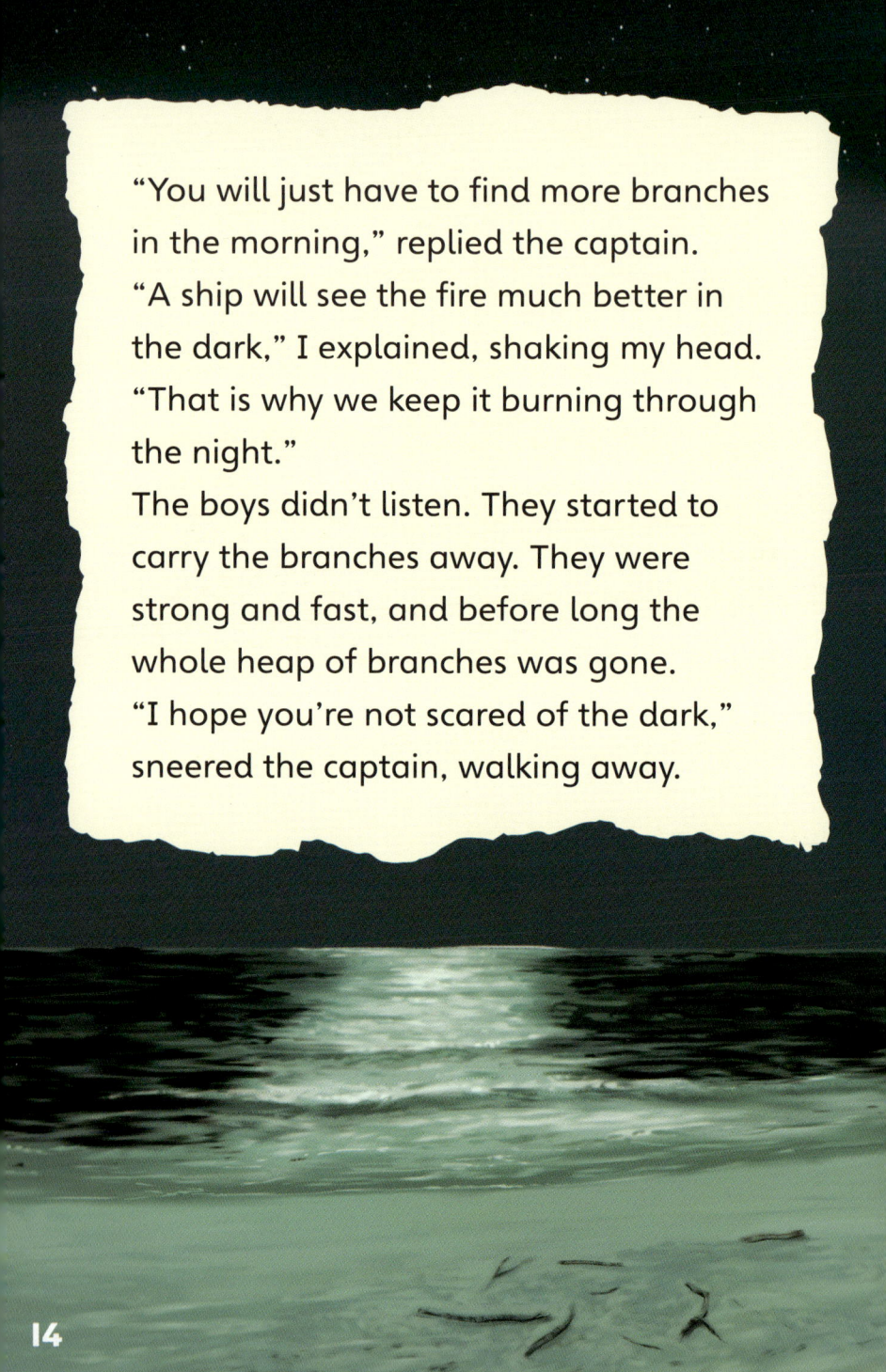

"You will just have to find more branches in the morning," replied the captain.
"A ship will see the fire much better in the dark," I explained, shaking my head. "That is why we keep it burning through the night."
The boys didn't listen. They started to carry the branches away. They were strong and fast, and before long the whole heap of branches was gone.
"I hope you're not scared of the dark," sneered the captain, walking away.

The orange fire was pale now.
It had nearly gone out.
"That was a stupid thing to do,"
I roared. "If a ship saw the fire, it
would rescue your team too."

Chapter Four

The Sport Squad boys vanished into the trees.
"Wait!" I yelled. "Come back!"
I could see something bright and shiny far out at sea.
"There's a ship!" I cried.

The Sport Squad boys sprinted back.
"Quick!" panted the captain, untying our rope. "Help us to signal to the ship."
We all ran up and down the beach and waved our arms, shouting loudly.
"It's hopeless," I said. "The ship will never see us without a fire."
Ricky tried to get the fire burning again, but it had gone out.

"Come on, Sport Squad. We are strong swimmers," said the captain, leaping into the waves. "If we swim fast, we might reach the ship."

His team splashed into the water behind him.

Ricky caught hold of my arm. "Don't follow them," he warned. "It's not safe to swim in the dark."

"I know," I said, pointing at the rough waves. "They have no chance of reaching the ship anyway. It's miles away."

The ship looked pale silver now as it vanished into the distance. I felt a sinking feeling in my stomach. Our chance of rescue had disappeared.

The Sport Squad boys swam back to the beach. They huddled together, shivering. The ship was gone now.

"Sorry," said the captain. "We should have kept the fire burning."

He swallowed nervously and looked at his feet in shame.

"It's down to us that everyone is still stuck on this island."

Ricky glared at him. "Well, go and fetch more branches to light another fire," he said coldly. "That's the least you can do."

The captain nodded. "From now on, things are going to be better," he said slowly. "From now on, I promise we'll work together as one team."

Ricky and I stared at him in surprise and disbelief.

"To show you that we're sorry," the captain said, "your team can share the meat we have for breakfast." Ricky was delighted when he heard about the food! I looked at the captain and smiled. If we really worked as one team, we could survive.

Quiz

Text detective

p3 — What evidence is there that Tariq is a wise captain?

p6 — How did Lena feel when she heard the noise?

p9–10 — How did the Sport Squad team overpower Lena and Ricky?

p13 — Why had Sport Squad tied up Lena and Ricky?

p13 — Why was Lena desperate when she learned of Sport Squad's plan?

p15 — Why was it foolish of Sport Squad to steal the firewood?

p18 — How would you describe Sport Squad's plan to swim out to the ship?

p19 — How does the Sport Squad captain feel?

p20 — What made the Sport Squad captain change his attitude?

p21 — What will be different on the island from now on?

What do you think?

How would you feel if you were Lena or Ricky? Could you forgive Sport Squad? Could you work with them as a team in the future?

Quiz

Text detective

- **p3** Which verb describes how the fire burns?
- **p8** How do we know that Lena is very scared?
- **p9** Which verb tells us that the attack was fast and sudden?
- **p11** How does the simile help you to picture the scene?
- **p15** Why is the speech verb 'roared' effective?
- **p19** Which expression tells us how Lena feels?
- **p20** Which adverb shows how angry Ricky is?

Vocabulary

- **p3** Find a word meaning 'stuck'.
- **p10** What does 'sneered' mean?
- **p13** Find a phrase that shows that Lena was astonished.
- **p17** Find a word meaning 'ran fast'.
- **p19** What does 'huddled' mean?

HA! HA!

Q: What is a shark's favourite game?

A: Swallow the leader!

Published by Pearson Education Limited, a company incorporated in England and Wales, having its registered office at Edinburgh Gate, Harlow, Essex, CM20 2JE.
Registered company number: 872828

www.pearsonschools.co.uk

Pearson is a registered trademark of Pearson plc

Text © Pearson Education Limited 2013

The right of Lou Kuenzler to be identified as the author of this work has been asserted by her in accordance with the Copyright, Designs and Patents Act 1988.

First published 2013

18 17
10 9 8 7 6 5

British Library Cataloguing in Publication Data is available from the British Library on request.

ISBN: 978 0 435 15258 1

Copyright notice
All rights reserved. No part of this publication may be reproduced in any form or by any means (including photocopying or storing it in any medium by electronic means and whether or not transiently or incidentally to some other use of this publication) without the written permission of the copyright owner, except in accordance with the provisions of the Copyright, Designs and Patents Act 1988 or under the terms of a licence issued by the Copyright Licensing agency, Saffron House, 6-10 Kirby Street, London EC1N 8TS (www.cla.co.uk). Applications for the copyright owner's written permission should be addressed to the publisher.

Designed by Bigtop
Original illustrations © Pearson Education Limited 2013
Illustrated by Nelson Evergreen
Printed in China (CTPS)
Font © Pearson Education Ltd
Teaching notes by Dee Reid

Acknowledgements
We would like to thank the following schools for their invaluable help in the development and trialling of this course:
Callicroft Primary School, Bristol; Castlehill Primary School, Fife; Elmlea Junior School, Bristol; Lancaster School, Essex; Llanidloes School, Powys; Moulton School, Newmarket; Platt C of E Primary School, Kent; Sherborne Abbey CE VC Primary School, Dorset; Upton Junior School, Poole; Whitmore Park School, Coventry.